Introducti

The Vale of Clwyd in Denbighshire is a k lying between the border and Snowdon area and easily accessible from the A55 expr which takes its name from the river Clwyd flowing through its length, nestles between the Clwydian Hills and gently rolling hills in the west. The Vale starts as a narrow enclosed river valley, then broadens into a fertile plain, passing the historic market towns of Denbigh, Ruthin and St Asaph to meet the coast at Rhyl.

It is the historic gateway into the hinterland of North Wales, and during the Middle Ages, became a contested borderland, subject to constant changes in influence and control from the Welsh Princes, the powerful Marcher Lords, and English monarchs.

In addition to its splendid scenery, the Vale contains a wealth of ancient and medieval sites, buildings and other treasures. These include iron-age settlements, Norman castles, the smallest cathedral in England and Wales, unique double-naved churches with intricately carved roofs, holy wells, and many fine houses of historical or architectural interest.

This new fully revised and extended edition contains 22 circular walks which explore rivers, wooded valleys, limestone crags, undulating farmland and low hills, and visit many of these places of interest, including enchanting old country inns. The routes, which range from 2½ to 7½ miles, follow public rights of way or permissive paths and are within the capability of most people. *A key feature is that most individual routes, as well as containing shorter walk options, can easily be linked with others, to provide longer day walks, if required.* This increases choice and encourages creativity in your walking routes. Walking boots are recommended, along with appropriate clothing to protect against the elements.

Each walk has a detailed map and description which enables the route to be followed without difficulty. Bear in mind though that changes in detail can occur at any time – eg. installation of additional stiles. The location of each walk is shown on the back cover and a summary of their key features is also given. This includes an estimated walking time, but allow more time to enjoy the scenery and sights.

Most walks are accessible via the Vale Rider bus network. Telephone Denbighshire County Council (01824 706968) for details or pick up a timetable at a local library. Please remember that the condition of paths can vary according to season and weather. Refer any path problems encountered to Denbighshire Highways Department – 01824 706872.

Please observe the Countryside Code.

Enjoy your walking!

WALK I

RIVER ELWY & ST ASAPH CATHEDRAL

DESCRIPTION A 3¼ mile (**A**) or 2 mile (**B**) walk featuring attractive riverside scenery, some of the sights of the City of St Asaph, and an opportunity to visit the Cathedral. Allow about 1½ hours.

START St Asaph Car Park [SJ 035743]

DIRECTIONS The car park and toilets are situated at the bottom of the High Street below the 16thC Parish Church and before Pont Elwy.

*S*t Asaph, or Llanelwy – 'the church by the river Elwy' – is a small cathedral city, whose roots lie in the monastery established here in about 560 by St Kentigern, originally from Scotland, and later run by his favourite pupil Asaph, a local man.

N

¼ mile

ST ASAPH

Cathedral

Pont Elwy

almshouses

Roe Plas

I From the north-west corner of the car park take the tarmaced path that passes to the left of the playground down to an information board by the river Elwy. Follow the path by the river past an information board to go under an arch of Elwy bridge, built about 1770, into Roe Plas Community Park. Continue ahead on a riverside path past an information board about the rare Black Poplars. Later bear LEFT behind the far end of the football pitch to reach an access lane which you follow back through the park to the road. Cross the road. *Here is the Mary Short Fountain, not in its original site, built in 1865 by Bishop Vowler Short in memory of his wife to provide a local water supply.* Go over the bridge and bear RIGHT with the road, then turn RIGHT along a lane past a surgery and go on to the embankment to begin a delightful 1¼ mile walk alongside the tree-lined river Elwy. It soon passes under the A55.

2 A little further you reach a small road bridge over the river. (For **Walk B** cross the bridge and follow the stiled riverside path back towards St. Asaph. Just before the A55 bridge turn left up a path to the road, to rejoin the main walk.) Continue along the western bank of the river. *Ahead lies Rhuddlan Castle, and to the west, Bodelwyddan, with its castle and marble church. The embankment on which you walk was built following severe flooding in 1963.* After just over ½ mile cross a footbridge over the river to a road. Turn RIGHT and follow this quiet country road back towards St. Asaph, passing 18thC Pen-y-Bryn and crossing the A55. When it bends right, keep ahead to follow a path past a cemetery then alongside a wall to rejoin the road. Follow it past a church, now a wildlife sanctuary, through the peaceful suburbs to a crossroads and the nearby Cathedral.

*T*he Cathedral is the smallest in England and Wales, and since its beginning in 1239, has had a chequered history, being burnt by Edward I's army in 1282, and again by Owain Glyndwr's Welsh troops in 1402. The present building dates from the 14thC and contains many interesting features. It

2

also houses early Welsh editions of the Bible and Prayer Book, which was first published in 1588. Bishop William Morgan, and other St. Asaph clergy were primarily responsible for the translation, which was crucial to the survival of the Welsh language. Their deeds are recorded on the Translators Memorial outside the cathedral.

Go down the High Street back to the start – at the bottom passing the Parish Church dating from 1524, and the Barrow almshouses built in 1686 to house eight local widows.

WALK 2

CEFN

DESCRIPTION A 5 mile walk which follows quiet country lanes and the few available link paths to explore the little known parish of Cefn Meiriadog, with its attractive wooded limestone ridges, old houses, churches, and good views. The walk passes the famous Pontnewydd Cave, where Early Stone Age hunters and gathers lived over 230,000 years ago. Allow about 2½ hours.
START Cae Onnen, near Glascoed [SH 998735].
DIRECTIONS From St. Asaph follow the B5381 west for about 3 miles. At a junction opposite Glascoed Lodge, take the road signposted Cefn Meiriadog /Llannefydd to find roadside parking at Cae Onnen on the right just before a junction.

*P*ontnewydd Cave is the earliest known human occupied site in Wales and the most north westerly site in Europe ½ million years ago. Excavations have revealed human remains, stone tools and the bones of wolf, bear, rhinocerous, bison and other animals.*

I Continue along the road, past the side road to Llannefydd, then take the right fork past All Saints Church, Sinan, which opened in 1875. Follow the road past Plas Newydd dating from 1583, enjoying good views over the Elwy valley. At a junction, turn LEFT past Ysgubor Newydd and follow the road beneath the wooded limestone ridge. At the next junction turn RIGHT. After about 300 yards take a signposted path on the right. It crosses the edge of a wooded limestone ridge, then steadily descends through the trees to the bottom of the wood, before passing through an area of young trees to the road. Turn LEFT to reach a junction. Continue up the road to pass the sealed entrance to Pontnewydd Cave up to your left. Follow the road round past the castellated community hall built in 1908.

2 At the junction, turn LEFT and follow the road past houses, with a good view of the parish church of St. Mary's built in 1863-4 on a prominent ridge overlooking the Vale. After about 400 yards, cross a ladder-stile on the right. Head half-LEFT down the field to eventually cross a stile in the bottom hedge. Turn LEFT up the road. At the junction, keep ahead and follow the road for about ¾ miles. At a bend near an old stone cottage, take a signposted path over a stile on the left. Go straight across two fields to cross a stile above a house. Turn RIGHT and follow the fence round to reach the driveway of Pentre Bach. Follow it down to the road. Turn LEFT and follow the road, later passing a chapel and a primary school, back to the start.

WALK 3

AROUND TREMEIRCHION & WAEN

DESCRIPTION A 6¼ mile walk (**A**) following mainly good field paths from the edge of the Clywdian Hills across the Vale, featuring historic houses, extensive open views and old country inns. Allow about 3½ hrs. The route includes a shorter 2¼ mile walk (**B**).

START Church of Corpus Christi, Tremeirchion [SJ 083731] or Farmer's Arms, Waen [SJ 062732]

DIRECTIONS In Tremeirchion, turn off the B5429, signposted to Holywell, to find roadside parking by the church, just below the Salusbury Arms. The Farmer's Arms, where parking is allowed, lies on a minor road between the A55 and Trefnant.

*T**he attractive** Church of Corpus Christi, dating mainly from the 14th and 15th centuries, has many ancient items of interest, including a C13th cross slab forming a seat in the porch, rare 17th century portrait glass, and an impressive canopied C14th tomb. Outside stands a yew tree reputed to be over 800 years old.*

I Continue up the road past the Salusbury Arms, a 14thC coaching inn, then just beyond a farm take a stepped path on the right. Go half-LEFT up the field to cross a stile by the entrance to a large house. Turn RIGHT down a green track to cross another stile. Turn RIGHT and follow the field boundary down to go through a gate at a good viewpoint. Now follow a stiled path down the right-hand edge of three fields to a road (caution). Turn LEFT, soon passing Ffynnon Beuno. *Named after the ancient stone healing well adjoining the house, it was a farmhouse and inn, when John Rowlands, later the famous explorer H.M.Stanley, stayed here with his aunt after leaving the workhouse at St. Asaph in 1856, before emigrating to America.* At the junction turn RIGHT.

2 Shortly, take a signposted path through a gate on the right. Now head half-LEFT across parkland – *soon with a good view of Brynbella, the 18thC mansion of Mrs Thrale, the travelling companion of the eminent writer, Dr. Samuel Johnson* – later crossing a stream to go through a waymarked gate by the stream in the far field corner. Go through the adjoining gate and across two fields to go through a gate near a large house and farm complex onto an access track. (For **Walk B**, turn right up the track, then right past farm buildings. Keep ahead along the drive towards two houses, and go through a facing gate at the end of the large wall. Go up the edge of two fields, and at a waymarked gatepost, go half-right to go through a waymarked gate. Follow the driveway left to the road. Turn right, then left up the road back to the start.)

3 For **Walk A**, turn LEFT to follow the track through a gate and across a stream, then go through a waymarked gate on the right. Head half-LEFT across the field to cross a stile/footbridge at the wood corner. Go up the wood edge, then at its corner go through the second (waymarked) gate. Continue down the long field, initially alongside the wood boundary, to go through a gate at the far end. Keep ahead to cross a stile in the bottom left-hand field corner. Go along the field edge, over a stile, then follow the stream through the next field to cross a stile onto an access lane. Follow it RIGHT up to a road. Turn LEFT along the road to cross a stile on the right. Cross a stile in the fence on your right about 100 yards ahead. Go half-LEFT to follow a stiled path up and across three fields to reach a stone stile at a wood corner by the road.

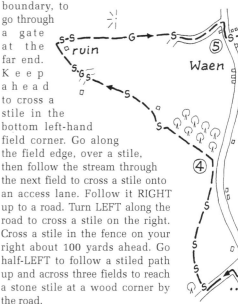

4 Turn LEFT and follow the field edge past the wood to cross a stile. Continue ahead alongside the boundary, past a house and on to cross a stile in the far corner. Go up the slope ahead and across the field towards a distant silo, later descending to a stile onto an access lane. Go through the gate almost opposite and on over a stile ahead. Follow the field edge to pass the ruin of Cil Owen – *reputedly where Owain Glyndŵr and his Welsh army rested during his struggle against the English forces in the early 15thC.* At the boundary corner turn RIGHT to cross a stile and then another by a water trough ahead. Go up the field edge – *with a good view looking back to St. Asaph* – to go through a gate in the corner. Continue across the next field to cross a stile onto a lane, which you follow to a junction. Turn RIGHT to reach the Farmer's Arms, an old coaching inn.

5 Cross a stile at the end of the inn. Continue down the field edge to cross a stile by a farm. Turn LEFT over the adjoining fence, go along the field edge and over a stile. Now follow the stiled path along the edge of three fields. After crossing a footbridge, head half-RIGHT across the large field to cross a stile in the far corner, and another stile/footbridge ahead. The path heads across the field towards a house, then at a small pond, it does almost a U-turn to angle down the field past a stile below to cross a stiled footbridge. Go half-RIGHT across the field corner to take a waymarked path across a footbridge/stile. Turn LEFT along the field edge and on to cross a stile in the far boundary. Now follow a stiled path through several fields to reach the road. Follow it RIGHT up into Tremeirchion. At the junction keep ahead, then at Ar Graig cross a stile on the left and follow the enclosed path up to a stile and on past a house and the nearby school to the start.

Ffynnon Beuno

TREMEIRCHION

Inn

N

walk B

Brynbella

Ffynnon Beuno

¼ mile

WALK 4

FOXHALL

DESCRIPTION A 6 mile walk (**A**) exploring the gently undulating countryside between Denbigh and Henllan, and its sites of historical interest, with good views. Highlights include medieval houses and church, an iron-age enclosure, and a haunted 13thC thatched inn in Henllan. Allow about 3 hours. A shorter 4½ mile walk (**B**) is included. The route can easily be undertaken in other shorter circuits by starting just outside Denbigh.

START Lenton Pool roundabout, Denbigh [SJ 050661] or a lay-by just outside Denbigh [SJ 043660] or alternatively Llindir Inn, Henllan [SJ 023681]

DIRECTIONS Lenton Pool is situated just west of the High Street by The Hand Inn. For the alternative Denbigh start, follow the A543 towards Pentrefoelas to find a parking area on the left, just after the road bends left at point **2**.

1 From Lenton Pool *(once a pond stocked with fish to be eaten by local people during Lent)* take the road towards Pentrefoelas. Before Morrisons turn up Glas Meadows Lane, then follow a path up to a road. Turn RIGHT, then LEFT into Llewelyns Estate. After about 100 yards, follow an enclosed path on the right, passing behind bungalows to reach a field. Follow the boundary on your left, and then go half-RIGHT across the next field to reach an access track leading to Galch Hill – *the historic home of the Myddelton family.* Turn RIGHT to cross a nearby stile on the right and head half-LEFT to join the boundary beyond the house, then go along the field edge to turn RIGHT over a stile. Follow the enclosed stiled path, then field path to reach the A543 by the alternative start.

2 Cross the road and go down the grass verge – *enjoying a good view of Denbigh Castle* – then follow the signposted path along the drive to Lodge Farm. Just before the splendid three storey stone house, cross a stile up on the left. Turn RIGHT along the boundary, then head half-LEFT to pass to the

left of outbuildings and follow an enclosed stiled path to a lane. Turn RIGHT and at the road cross a stone stile on the left.

3 Go half-RIGHT across two fields to enter a wood. Follow the waymarked path through the attractive woodland – *full of bluebells in the spring.* After passing through a second gate follow the path through a wall/ fence gap, then follow the waymarked trees on your right to cross a stile near the boundary wall of Foxhall. *En route, look for the low banks of an iron-age enclosure to your right by a clump of trees. Foxhall was originally a single storey, semi-fortified hall house, where once lived Sir Humphrey Llwyd – a 16thC cartographer, author, physician, musician, M.P. known as the father of modern geography.* Continue ahead to the large stone wall and a stile in the corner. (For **Walk B**, follow the wall left to a gateway in it, then head half-left across a track to cross a stile in the field corner. Go half-right through a wood to a stile. Turn right along the field, over a stile, then turn left to go past farm buildings, through a small gate and along another field. Go through two gates and up the field, through a gate, and on up the next field to go through a gate on the right. Turn left down the field and follow the stiled path to a lane. Turn left to point **6**.)

4 Cross the stile, and follow the edge of a large field. *To the left are the ruins of Foxhall Newydd – a three storey building commenced by John Panton, Recorder of Denbigh, in the late 16thC. It was to be the largest house in the area, but unfortunately he went bankrupt and it was never completed.* After crossing a stile continue along an enclosed path, then a field path behind hous-

HENLLAN
Llindir
Inn ⑤

es to a lane. Turn RIGHT to reach the main road in Henllan. Follow it LEFT through the village, then go up Church Road to the Church of St Sadwrn. *This fine medieval church has a detached 15thC tower, reputedly built to ensure that its bells could be heard throughout a parish once 16 miles long. Note the remains of an old preaching cross and font outside the porch.* Leave the churchyard by the lower gate to reach the road opposite the Llindir Inn, where refreshments are available. *This inn dating from 1229, named from the llin (flax) once grown locally, is reputed to be haunted by Sylvia, murdered by her husband, a sea captain and former landlord.*

5 Go up the lane past the inn, then turn RIGHT to pass in front of a house (Hireathog) to cross a stile to the left of a garage into a field. Go ahead to walk on the left of a short section of hedge, and on downhill to cross a footbridge over a stream. Continue ahead along the field edge to cross a stile. Head half-LEFT to cross a stile in the tree boundary. Turn RIGHT and follow the boundary, soon bending LEFT to cross a stile in the field corner onto an old enclosed path. Follow it LEFT past a stile to cross a footbridge over a stream. Continue on the enclosed path up to join a hedge-lined track. Follow it to houses and continue along their access drive.

6 Cross a cattle grid at the entrance to Tan y Marian and an adjoining stile. Go along the edge of two fields to cross footbridges/stiles in the boundary ahead. Go up the field, past a telegraph pole and on over a stile in the boundary and another just ahead. Now go half-LEFT down the field, over a stile and on in the same direction to reach the road. Follow it LEFT back down into Denbigh, enjoying good views of the castle.

7

WALK 5

AROUND THE YSTRAD VALLEY

DESCRIPTION A delightful figure of eight 6¼ mile walk **(A)** exploring the wooded Ystrad valley, and the attractive undulating countryside around Denbigh. The route visits several historic houses, including Gwaenynog, renowned for its association with Dr. Johnson and Beatrice Potter. Allow about 3 hours. The route can easily be shortened to a 4 mile walk **(B)** in the Lawnt. Also, by using the initial route of Walk 4 to Galch Hill as shown you can create an enjoyable 3¾ mile walk to Gwaenynog or make an alternative return to Denbigh.
START Library, High Street, Denbigh [SJ 053661].

I Go up Bull Lane past the side of the Bull Hotel, then go through the wall gap on the first bend, and follow the path down to the end of the handrail. *Here is a fine view over Howell's School – a renowned independent girls school which was opened in 1859 by the Drapers Company – a City of London Guild, from a trust legacy left by Thomas Howell, a 16thC Welsh merchant member of the company.* Turn RIGHT down to Howell's perimeter fence and follow it beneath the old town walls, past a tower, and along the wood edge to go through a kissing gate on the left and another just ahead. Go half-LEFT down the field to cross a stile in the corner by a kissing gate. Continue through the edge of four fields to cross a stile in the last field corner. Follow a narrow enclosed path to a road.

2 Go down the road, then take a signposted path through a gate on the right. Go across a footbridge over the river, past a ruin, then bear LEFT up to a stile and on up a field to a lane at Pen-y-Banc. Cross a stile on the right at the end of converted outbuildings. Go along the field edge, and, at the next field, go half-LEFT to cross a stile in the corner. Go ahead up the field edge and through

a gate, then continue alongside a wall. At its end, bend LEFT through a gateway and follow a gated green track through two fields to a stony cross-track. Follow it RIGHT past farm buildings. Where the lower access track bends left, go through a gate on the right, and on to a gateway near the front of Segrwyd Hall. *The Hall and estate, first recorded in 1343, were given to Richard Dolben by Henry VIII in 1493, as a reward for his support, and remained with his family until the late 18thC, after which the Hall was completely re-built. Later occupants have included Susannah Mostyn, a keen photographer, and Price Edward Storey, a wealthy brewer, who had a special 'sleeper' railway carriage to transport him to South Downs sheep shows.*

3 Here take a waymarked path down through a narrow wooded valley above a stream to a driveway. Follow it LEFT to the road at the Lawnt – *the site of an old fulling mill used in the manufacture of woollen cloths. Still working in Victorian times, it produced a roll of cloth sent to Prince Albert as a wedding gift.* Follow the road RIGHT. (For **Walk B**, just past Lawnt Cottage take a path on the right, resuming the text at point **6**.) Continue along the road.

4 Shortly, turn sharp LEFT on a signposted enclosed path, soon passing behind a house. Continue through the valley, soon following the river past a footbridge to a stile. Follow the path past a ruin, through a clearing, over a stile and on through a small wood. *In the next field, down by the river, is a monument erected in honour of Dr. Samuel Johnson, an eminent writer and early compiler of the English dictionary, who stayed with Colonel John*

8

Myddelton at Gwaenynog during a tour of North Wales in 1774. His travelling companion Mrs Thrale, observed 'here we are loved, esteemed and honoured'. Return through the wood, and just before the stile, angle sharp LEFT up to enter a field. Go up the field edge to cross a stile by a pool in the trees. Follow a track bearing LEFT to a gate. Keep ahead to cross a stile and another one further ahead.

5 Go along the field near the large wall to a stile and on to reach the driveway of nearby Gwaenynog. *Dating from the 16thC, it has been the home of two important local families – the Middletons and the Burtons. Beatrix Potter , the niece of Frederick Burton, spent her childhood holidays here, and it was its beautiful garden that inspired her classic children's book 'Tale of the Flopsy Bunnies'.* Follow the track opposite across two fields. *Soon Denbigh Castle appears.* Continue down the edge of the next two fields to the part timber-framed house of Galch Hill (*the birth-place of Sir Hugh Myddelton, who provided London with its first water supply, and of Sir*

Thomas Myddelton, who became Lord Mayor of London). (A stile further down offers a more direct route back to Denbigh as shown.) Here turn RIGHT to descend the field to the road. Follow it RIGHT then cross a stile on the left just before Lawnt Cottage.

6 Go along the field past a house, through a gate, and on through the Ystrad valley. Cross a stile and another just above the river. Take the path rising half-LEFT and follow the main path through the wooded valley. Go through a small gate and on past a house to follow its access track to the road. Follow the road LEFT, past the former North Wales Hospital – *which provided services for the mentally ill from 1848 until 1995.* At a junction, continue ahead, then turn RIGHT to follow a road beneath the castle walls, and on past Leicester's Church back to the start.

WALK 6
DENBIGH CASTLE

DESCRIPTION This interesting 2½ mile walk takes you from the attractive hamlet of Brookhouse on field paths to one of the most impressive, but least well known castles in Wales, and explores the old fortified walled town of Denbigh. It involves a short steep climb to the castle, with an easier route available. It can equally be walked from Denbigh Castle, which has its own car park. Allow about 2 hours. The walk can be combined with a visit to the castle and a walk along the old town walls – one of Denbigh's hidden gems (a key is available from the Castle custodian or the Library).
START Brookhouse Mill [SJ 072658] or Denbigh Castle [SJ 052658]
DIRECTIONS From Denbigh, head towards Ruthin on the A525, to park in a lay-by alongside the Brookhouse Mill, or alternatively park by the river in Brookhouse. Denbigh Castle is signposted from the town centre.

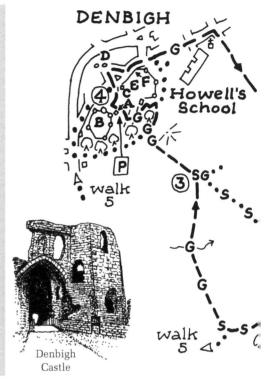

Denbigh Castle

*D*enbigh *(Dinbych), meaning 'little fortress', developed as a key border town during the Middle Ages, becaming an important power base for Welsh princes in their struggles against the Marcher Lords and English kings. By 1282 Edward I had taken Denbigh and conquered North Wales. Built between 1282 and 1310, Denbigh Castle, with its strong enclosure wall defended by seven towers and a mighty gatehouse, and integral walled town, was one of the largest of a chain of castles commissioned by Edward, to enforce English control of the heartland of North Wales. The fortified town was settled by English immigrants, mainly families from estates in northern England. By 1586, the town, with an inadequate water supply, and vulnerable to attack, had been deserted by its inhabitants, in favour of a developing town further downhill. The castle itself survived other turbulent periods, until the Civil War, when the Royalist garrison surrendered after a six month siege in 1646. After this the castle fell into ruin.*

I Go past the front of the Brookhouse Mill, a converted 17thC watermill, through an underpass beneath the A525 into Brookhouse. *The cottages were built by John Mostyn for his workers about 1750. One of his former woollen mills is now occupied by the renowned potters David and Margaret Ffrith, and is worth a visit.* Continue along the road alongside the river Ystrad, and just past a weir, cross a stile on the left. Follow the river to pass under an old railway bridge – *the former Denbigh – Corwen line (1864 -1962).* Now go half-RIGHT to follow a path through four fields to a road. Turn LEFT. (or cross the stile opposite to follow a waymarked stiled path to point **3**). Just before the bridge over the river cross a stile on the right.

2 Follow the path along the edge of three fields, skirting a small wood and descending to a stile. Follow the path up to cross a stile in the right-hand corner of the next field. Go along the field edge, through a gate and along the edge of the next two fields to cross a stile at a path junction. *This section provides good views of Denbigh Castle on its wooded hilltop, and of Howell's School, a renowned independent girls school. It was*

commemorative plaque marks the location). For five years this was his home, cared for by his grandfather. After the latter's death, he was placed with the church sexton at the cottage (no.63) **(A)** *you pass.*

It was from here that he was taken, aged six years, to the workhouse in St. Asaph – a journey that later took him to America and subsequent world fame. He made several later visits to Denbigh, the castle's visitor's book recording one in 1866.

opened in 1859 by the Drapers Company – a City of London Guild, from a trust legacy left by Thomas Howell, a 16thC Welsh merchant member of the company.

3 Head half-LEFT up the next field. Go through two kissing gates to reach a path by the wood edge. (Turning left, then following roads to the castle is the easy option.) A more intriguing approach is to turn RIGHT alongside the perimeter fence. About 30 yards before one of the castle towers, turn LEFT to go up a flight of steps. Now follow a delightful zig-zag path up through the trees, over an access drive, and up steps to suddenly emerge on an open green by the castle car park. Head LEFT towards the castle **(B)** entrance. *H. M. Stanley, the renowned explorer, of 'Dr. Livingstone, I presume?' fame, was born in 1841, in a small cottage in front of the castle, long since demolished (a*

4 After visiting the castle, and the town walls, head half-RIGHT down to pass to the left of St. Hilary's Tower **(C)** – *all that remains of the garrison church built in the early 14thC and demolished in 1923.* Continue down the road straight ahead to the impressive Burgess Gate **(D)** – *the main entrance to the medieval walled town.* Now head east along a walkway offering panoramic views over the town. Near the road junction and the entrance to the town walls **(F)** stands Leicester's Church **(E)**. *Begun in 1578 by the Earl of Leicester, possibly as a replacement for St. Asaph Cathedral, it was never finished due to lack of finance and local opposition.* Follow the road down, and when it bends left, go through a wall-gap ahead and follow a path down to the entrance to Howell's. Continue down the lane. At the far end of the church, turn RIGHT along an enclosed path past sports fields, then follow a kissing-gated path along the edge of three fields to a road. Follow the road RIGHT, then at the next junction, turn LEFT. Now simply follow the quiet country road back to the start, perhaps visiting the pottery or enjoying refreshments at the Brookhouse Mill.

ST DYFNOG'S CHURCH TO LLWYN WOOD

DESCRIPTION A 6¾ mile walk exploring the attractive varied countryside between Llanrhaeadr and the hamlet of Brookhouse. Highlights include St. Dyfnog's medieval church, with its famous Jesse window, and Holy Well and Bath, old almhouses, two potteries, ancient woodland, two miles of riverside walking, and good open views. Allow about 3½ − 4 hours. Refreshments are available at a 16thC coaching inn in Llanrhaeadr and a 17thC converted watermill in Brookhouse. The route can easily be shortened to a 4½ mile (**B**) or 4¾ mile (**C**) walk from the respective starts using the good stiled link field path as shown.

START St. Dyfnog's Church, Llanrhaeadr [SJ 082634] or alternatively, Brookhouse Mill [SJ 072658]

DIRECTIONS From Denbigh, head towards Ruthin on the A525. After 2 miles turn right to Llanrhaeadr. Park on an old section of road on the right, or in the village itself. See **Walk 8** for the alternative start.

*S*t *Dyfnog's Church*, dating from the 13thC, and rebuilt in the 16thC, is a medieval Welsh church of great renown. Undoubtedly its greatest treasure is the Tree of Jesse window (1533), probably the finest medieval stained glass window in Wales. During the Civil War, it was buried in the woods in the chest that now lies below it, and restored in 1660. In the churchyard is the grave of Ann Parry. Just before she died in 1787, she said that God had told her that her body would remain as uncorruptible as her soul. 43 years later, when her her son was buried in the same grave, the coffin fell open to reveal her perfectly preserved. On her gravestone is written 'God kept his word'!

I On leaving the church by the lychgate opposite Anvil Pottery (*sited in the old smithy*) turn LEFT alongside the wall to enter the churchyard by a small gate. Go past old almhouses − *built in 1729, by Jane Jones for poor elderly people of the parish, and still in use today* − and through an arched doorway into a wooded valley. Follow a well-used and popular local path RIGHT alongside a stream to reach St Dyfnog's Well and Bath. *Tradition has it that St. Dyfnog lived here in the 6thC, and that for penance, he stood under the small waterfall. This gave the water healing properties, and it became a celebrated holy well, visited by many pilgrims. In the 18thC the bath was paved with marble and surrounded by bathing rooms. Only the bath and waterfall remain.* Follow the path up through the trees to pass through a wall-gap. Turn RIGHT through gateposts to reach the driveway to the nearby vicarage. Follow it LEFT, then go through a gate on your right. Go up the field edge to cross a stile in the field corner, and on through the edge of a wood to a road. Turn LEFT, then go up the signposted path on the right to cross a stile.

2 Go ahead across the golf course to a tall waymarker post near a tree-enclosed tennis court to reach further golf links. Head almost half-LEFT up to a wood corner, then follow the waymarked path along the wood boundary to cross a stile by the fifth tee. Follow a path through the corner of the wood to reach a track by a waymarker post. Follow it RIGHT to enter Coed Mawr. Shortly, follow the waymarked path LEFT along another track. It then angles half-RIGHT off the track, soon descending to leave the wood by a stile. Keep ahead to follow the bottom field edge above a quarry to a road junction. Go ahead along the road signposted to Denbigh. At a junction, turn RIGHT.

3 At a junction by houses follow the signposted path opposite down the field edge to cross a stile just past a bungalow. Turn LEFT to follow the boundary round to cross a stile in the field corner. Turn LEFT and follow the boundary round to pass through a gate in the far field corner. Go along the edge of two fields to cross a stile onto a track. Follow it past the pond by Ystrad Farm, then go along its driveway to the road. Follow it RIGHT down the edge of

Ystrad valley. (For **Walk B**, cross a stile on the right just before the bridge, and follow a direct stiled path back to Llanrhaeadr.) After crossing over the river take a signposted path on the right through four fields to pass under an old railway bridge to reach a road. Follow it RIGHT alongside the river past Brookhouse Pottery and cottages, then go through an underpass to reach Brookhouse Mill.

4 Turn RIGHT along the road over the river, to cross a stile on the left. Follow the field edge past a private footbridge, and on to cross another gated bridge over the river. Turn RIGHT, and after 50 yards cross a stile on your left. Now follow a stiled riverside path to a road. Follow it RIGHT.

5 At a bridge over the river Clwyd, go down the signposted path. Now follow the stiled path near the river for almost a mile. At a bridge over the river, follow the track leading half-RIGHT, crossing a stream, then a disused railway line via stiles and on through a field and Llwyn Wood. *This ancient broadleaved woodland, an SSSI, acquired in 1998 by the Coed Cadw Woodland Trust, is the most significant remaining example of a wetland habitat once widespread in the Vale. A kissing gate allows*

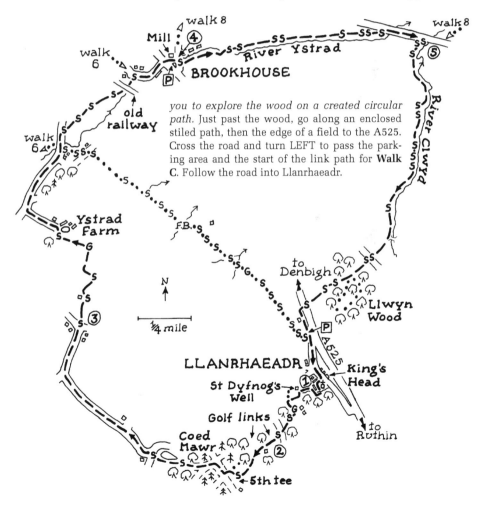

*you to explore the wood on a created circular path. Just past the wood, go along an enclosed stiled path, then the edge of a field to the A525. Cross the road and turn LEFT to pass the parking area and the start of the link path for **Walk C**. Follow the road into Llanrhaeadr.*

ST MARCELLA'S & LLEWENI HALL

DESCRIPTION This delightful 6-mile walk takes you to the Vale's finest medieval church, St. Marcella's (*open the first Saturday 10.00 – noon, April to October, or by prior arrangement with the Parish Office – telephone 01745 812284*), and then past the historic Lleweni Hall, before returning alongside the attractive rivers Clwyd and Ystrad. Allow about 3 hours.

START Brookhouse Mill, Brookhouse, near Denbigh [SJ 072658]

DIRECTIONS From Denbigh, head towards Ruthin on the A525, to park in a lay-by alongside the Brookhouse Mill.

I Follow the minor road past Brookhouse Mill – *a converted 17thC watermill.* On the bend take the signposted path past the side of the chapel, along the edge of two fields towards the church tower, then along an enclosed path to reach a road by St. Marcella's Church. *Denbigh's parish church is known locally as Whitchurch. Built on the site of a holy well and hermitage established by Marchell the Virgin in the 7thC, the present largely 15thC church is regarded as the jewel of churches in the Vale. Double-naved with an imposing tower, and large windows that lighten an impressive interior, the church has fine carved hammer-beamed roofs and contains monuments to the area's famous dignitaries. In the south altar area – once the private chapel of the Salusbury family of nearby Lleweni Hall – stands a splendid painted alabaster tomb of Sir John Salusbury and his wife Dame Jane. In the churchyard is the grave of Twm o'r Nant, the Welsh poet and actor.* After visiting the church continue along the right-hand side of the road with care for ¼ mile.

2 Opposite Kilford Farm, turn LEFT on a signposted path along an access lane, which you follow for nearly 1½ miles. *The lane offers excellent open views: to the west, St. Marcella's, and Denbigh Castle on its wooded hilltop overlooking the town; to the east, the Clwydian Hills – Moel y Parc with its TV. mast, running south to Penycloddiau and Moel Arthur crowned by iron-age hill-forts, then the ridge rising to Moel Famau, the highest point in the range, with its ruined Jubilee Tower. Eventually, you arrive at the entrance drive to Lleweni Hall. Nearby are the stables and coach house dating from 1735, which, like the Hall, are Grade II listed buildings. These replaced earlier stables and barracks, used during the Civil War by a large army of men and horses provided by Thomas Salusbury in support of the King. The buildings are being converted into luxury homes.*

3 *Lleweni's history dates back to 729 AD when Machweithiau, Chief of one of the 15 Noble Tribes of Wales, built a house here, later occupied by Prince David, Lord of Denbigh. The original Lleweni Hall was the seat of the Salusburys – one of the great families of North Wales – whose founding member came to this country with William the Conqueror. Work on the hall began in the late 1100s and it became one of the greatest houses in Wales. The Salusburys remained here until the late 1600s.*

Perhaps one of the most colourful characters ever to occupy Lleweni was Katheryn of Berain. The daughter of Tudor ap Robert Vychan of Berain, near Henllan, and a cousin of Queen Elizabeth, she was a renowned beauty, who was married to John Salusbury from 1557 until his death in 1566. They had two sons: John, a royalist, poet, friend and patron of Shakespeare, who is reputed to have once stayed at Lleweni, and Tom, who was implicated in an attempted overthrow of Elizabeth I, and was subsequently beheaded. Katherine later married a further three wealthy local gentry – Richard Clough, Maurice Wynn, and Edward Thelwall. Her six children, numerous step-children and grandchildren, who became the foundation of great families of Wales, earned her the name of 'Mam Cymru' – 'Mother of Wales'.

In 1774, the eminent Dr. Samuel Johnson and his travelling companion, Mrs Thrale, spent three weeks at Lleweni, enjoying the hospitality of her cousin Robert Cotton, who arranged visits to local places of interest. In

1785, the then owner, Thomas Fitzmaurice, established a bleach works nearby for treating linen produced on his Irish estates, and sold in Chester. He subsequently became bankrupt.

In 1810, Lleweni was bought by Rev. Edward Hughes of Kimnel, whose vast wealth was made from copper mining on Parys Mountain, Anglesey. Between 1816-18, his son, Thomas, the future Lord Dinorben, took down the wings of the Hall to enhance the family home at Kimnel. Reasons given are that he wanted to impress Queen Victoria on an anticipated visit to Kimnel which did not materialise, or 'in pique' because his wife refused to live at Lleweni! Either way it led to the wanton destruction of a magnificent building.

Continue along the lane.

St Marcella's

4 After crossing a bridge over the river Clwyd, bear RIGHT to begin a delightful section of riverside walking. The stiled path follows the course of the river through a series of fields for just over 2 miles to eventually reach a road. Turn RIGHT and follow the road for about ¼ mile, and at Pont Parc Canol cross a stile on the left to gain the bank of the river Ystrad. Now follow a stiled path alongside the river to reach a farm track. Follow it RIGHT to cross a gated bridge over the river. Turn RIGHT to walk near the river to reach the road by Brookhouse Mill, where refreshments are available.

N

¼ mile

Lleweni Hall

River Clwyd

St Marcella's church

to Denbigh

Kilford Farm

chapel

Mill

Pont Parc Canol

River Ystrad

walk 7

walks 6+7

BROOKHOUSE

to Ruthin

15

ST CWYFAN'S TRAIL

DESCRIPTION A delightful 6 mile walk (**A**) in the attractive countryside north of Llandyrnog. The route meanders through open country, past an 17thC farm, before rising to skirt the edge of the Clwydian Hills, with good views, to visit St Cwyfan's, the smallest medieval church in the Vale, at Llangwyfan. It returns to Llandyrnog which offers a choice of good country inns. Allow about 3½ hours. The route offers a shorter 4½ mile walk (**B**).

START St. Tyrnog's Church, Llandyrnog [SJ 108651]

DIRECTIONS Llandyrnog lies on the B5429 Bodfari – Llanbedr D.C. road. Parking is limited in the village centre, so at the cross-roads, turn towards Llangynhafal (Gladstone Terrace), then right into Nant Glyd, which offers some roadside parking. Walk along the lane opposite past the churchyard, then turn left to reach the church entrance.

The late medieval church of St Tyrnog's, standing by The White Horse Inn, contains the rare and only surviving stained glass 'Seven Sacrament' window in Wales. A key is available.

I From the church, cross the road and follow it RIGHT to cross a stile just before the school. Follow the school boundary, go over a stile, keep alongside the hedge then head half-RIGHT to cross a stile and footbridge in the field corner. Go along the field edge, over a stile, then half-way along the next field, cross a stile on the left. Continue along a track past houses, then cross a road to go along the driveway opposite past Hafan Awel. Just before a cattle-grid, cross a stile and head half-LEFT to cross a stile near the far wood corner. Follow a waymarked path through the wood, over a footbridge, then bearing RIGHT past the end of a pond and on to cross a footbridge and stile into a field. Head towards the house opposite and walk alongside its boundary wall. At its corner, turn LEFT across the field to the far boundary, then follow it RIGHT to a lane. Turn LEFT along the lane (For **Walk B**, after a cottage, turn right on a signposted path to follow field paths up to point **3**). Go past Pentre Mawr – *a 17thC working farm. The large red-bricked barn dates from the early 18thC. Note its distinctive bell tower and weather vane. This bell was used to call farm workers in for their meals.*

2 When the lane bends left becoming a track, take the signposted path through the gate ahead. Go along the field edge past a small pond to cross a stile on the left. Follow the boundary on your right round to go through an old gateway into another field. Keep ahead, go over a stile and through a small wood to cross a large footbridge and stile, then go across a field to a road. Follow it RIGHT to the B5429. Follow the road opposite up to Berth Farm. At outbuildings, turn RIGHT along a track past a house and follow it up through a gate to eventually cross a stile near an old farm. Bear half-LEFT up to a stile in the field corner. Continue alongside a fence to cross a stile, and follow the field boundary past a house to a lane. Turn RIGHT, then shortly RIGHT again down another lane.

3 On the bend, go through a gate on the left. Walk along the bottom edge of three fields, then half-way through the next field, cross a stile on the right. Now head half-LEFT down to another stile, then go along the edge of the next two fields, through a small wood, then beneath a house to reach a lane. Turn LEFT, then shortly go RIGHT over a cattle grid along a track. After 150 yards, head RIGHT down the large field to cross a stile in the hedge. Turn LEFT to follow a part-paved path towards Llangwyfan – *regularly walked by patients undergoing treatment at the complex of buildings which once was a TB. Sanatorium hospital.* Pass through a gate and go up a track to St Cwyfan's church. *Note the stocks. This 15thC church is situated on the old pilgrim's route from Holywell to St David's. Its simple Georgian interior remains unspoilt. By the entrance*

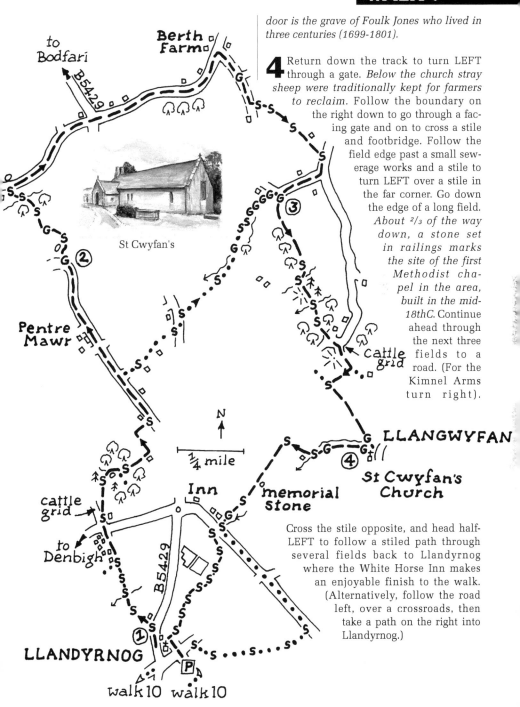

door is the grave of Foulk Jones who lived in three centuries (1699-1801).

4 Return down the track to turn LEFT through a gate. *Below the church stray sheep were traditionally kept for farmers to reclaim.* Follow the boundary on the right down to go through a facing gate and on to cross a stile and footbridge. Follow the field edge past a small sewerage works and a stile to turn LEFT over a stile in the far corner. Go down the edge of a long field. *About ²/₃ of the way down, a stone set in railings marks the site of the first Methodist chapel in the area, built in the mid-18thC.* Continue ahead through the next three fields to a road. (For the Kimnel Arms turn right).

Cross the stile opposite, and head half-LEFT to follow a stiled path through several fields back to Llandyrnog where the White Horse Inn makes an enjoyable finish to the walk. (Alternatively, follow the road left, over a crossroads, then take a path on the right into Llandyrnog.)

to Bodfari

B5429

Berth Farm

St Cwyfan's

Pentre Mawr

2

cattle grid

to Denbigh

B5429

Inn

memorial stone

N

¼ mile

LLANDYRNOG

walk 10   walk 10

3

cattle grid

LLANGWYFAN

4

St Cwyfan's Church

1

P

From the cross-roads in the centre of Llandyrnog take the road signposted to Llanrhaeadr. Follow it out of the village, past a staggered junction by a converted chapel, and on for another ½ mile to reach a bridge over the river Clwyd. Cross a stile on the left and follow the river through seven fields to reach another road. *Look out for herons and other wildfowl.* Turn LEFT to cross a stile on the right. Continue ahead, then shortly, angle away from the river across the field corner to cross a stile/footbridge in the boundary ahead. Go past the garden of a nearby house then along the edge of a large field to go through a gate on your right just before the corner. Head towards the field corner by the river to cross two stiles and a footbridge. Walk alongside the river. Shortly, cross a driveway by a bridge, then continue along a field by the river In the next field head half-LEFT, go through a gate and follow the boundary on your left round to cross a stile by the entrance to 17thC St Hychan's church.

2 Turn LEFT along the road to cross a stile on the right opposite the former school and teacher's house, dating from 1866. Follow the enclosed path to its end, then go along the edge of three fields to reach a road. (For **Walk B** follow the road left to the White Horse Inn at Hendrerwydd , and on to resume the text at point **5**.) Turn RIGHT into Gellifor village. At a junction, turn LEFT then go past the front of the school and along a lane. At a junction turn LEFT, then at a chapel, turn RIGHT along a lane to its end. Now follow a delightful tree-lined bridleway alongside a stream up to a road. Go through a hidden bridle gate opposite and continue up the bridleway to emerge on the lower slopes of the Clwydian Hills. After passing through a bridle gate, head half-LEFT up to cross a stile by a gate – *a nearby seat provides a stopping place with views* – and on to a lane.

3 Follow it LEFT down to St. Cynhafal's church. *This late 15thC double-naved church stands in a circular Celtic churchyard, against the backdrop of Moel Famau. It is the only church dedicated to this 7thC Welsh monk, whose holy well was renowned*

for treating warts and rheumatism. Its interior contains many interesting features, including a fine carved roof, and painted swan-like pelican on her nest above the south altar. A visit is recommended and a key can be obtained from the farm opposite. Above the church is the timber-framed house of Plas-yn-Llan, where the poet William Wordworth twice stayed in the 1790s. He was a college friend of the owner's son – Robert Jones – with whom he had shared a walking tour of Europe in 1790. Continue down the road to staggered cross-roads – *note the stocks.* Turn RIGHT, soon reaching Llangynhafal, with its 17thC Golden Lion Inn.

4 Take the Llandyrnog road opposite the inn. After passing signposted path on your right, take one on the LEFT through a gate.

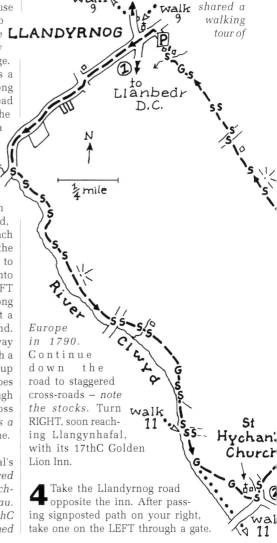

LLANDYRNOG

to Bodfari
walk 9
walk 9

to Llanbedr D.C.

N

¼ mile

River Clwyd

walk 11

St Hychan Church

walk 11

WALK 10

IN SEARCH OF ST CYNHAFAL

DESCRIPTION A delightful 6½ mile (**A**) walk exploring the attractive countryside lying between the river Clwyd and the lower slopes of the Clwydian Hills, south of Llandyrnog. The route follows riverside and field paths, a delightful old bridleway and quiet lanes, rising to the lovely remote 15thC church of St. Cynhafal and passing through peaceful hamlets. It provides good views and the opportunity to visit old country inns at Llangynhafal and Hendrerwydd (Tel: 01824 790451 and 790218 to check respective opening times). Allow about 4 hours. The route can easily be undertaken as two shorter walks of 4¾ miles (**B**) from Llandyrnog and 2¾ miles (**C**) from Llangynhafal.

START Llandyrnog [SJ 109651] or alternatively Llangynhafal [SJ 129635]

DIRECTIONS Llandyrnog lies on the B5429 Bodfari – Llanbedr D.C. road. See **Walk 9**. For the alternative start in Llangynhafal, parking is allowed at the Golden Lion.

Continue ahead, over a stile, and down the edge of the next long field to go through a gate. Follow a track then lane between two houses, bending half-RIGHT past Tyn-y-Pistyll to soon reach a road. Turn RIGHT. (For **Walk C** or a drink at the White Horse Inn in Hendrerwydd, turn LEFT.)

5 Cross a stile on the left and a fence opposite. Go down the edge of the long narrow field to pass to the left of two facing gateways. Now go across the middle of the field to cross a stile in the far field corner. Go up the field edge and across the next large field to a hidden stile in the recessed corner ahead. Continue along the next field edge, past a house and on down to a road. Turn RIGHT, then cross a stile on the left. Go up the field and into the next to cross adjoining stiles/fences in the corner. Continue ahead, initially alongside the boundary to cross a stile in the hedge ahead. Follow the boundary on your left to go through the second of two gates on the left. Continue along the field edge to cross a stile/footbridge and follow a path between houses to emerge in a small housing estate. Go up the road back to the start.

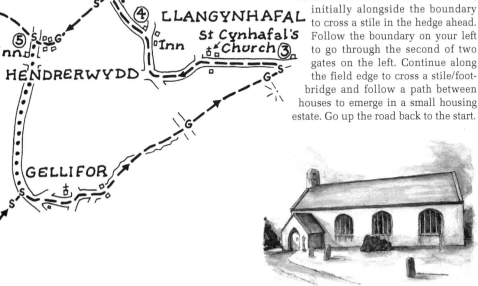

St Cynhafal's

WALK II
WITH
ST CHRISTOPHER'S
BLESSING

DESCRIPTION A delightful 4-mile walk featuring attractive sections of the rivers Clywedog and Clwyd. The route takes you from Rhewl to the hamlet of Llanynys, to visit one of the most interesting ancient churches in the Vale – St. Saeran's (usually open during daylight hours), containing the finest medieval wall painting in North Wales. It later passes by one of the Vale's historic houses or follows an alternative route back to Rhewl. The popular Drovers Arms, with its traditional ales and good daily food, makes a fine ending to the walk. Allow about 2½ hours.
START Drovers Arms, Rhewl [SJ 109604].
DIRECTIONS The Drovers Arms, where parking is allowed, lies on the A525 Denbigh – Ruthin road at Rhewl.

The Drovers Arms was once an important stopping place for drovers. The pine trees behind the inn were a traditional marker used to guide them to this place of refuge. Cattle were housed at the farm opposite. The inn is reputedly haunted – just ask the landlord! Nearby is Capel Rhewl and its minister's house, where once lived Emyrs ap Iwan, a famous Welsh methodist minister and bard.

Follow the A525 towards Denbigh past the school and after the last house, take a signposted path over a stile on the right. Turn LEFT and follow the field edge round to cross a stile in the far corner by the river. Follow the stiled riverside path through an enclosed section, and along the edge of two fields, then past a small pond and through a small enclosure to go through a small gate into a large field. Go along the field edge, and after about 160 yards, cross a stile in the boundary, and another just ahead. Continue near the river, over a stile and along the riverside edge of a long field past a bridge.

In the field corner cross a gate and continue beside the river to pass through a gate at a stone-arched bridge. Turn RIGHT through the adjoining gate and follow a track through the edge of three fields to its end, where you cross a stream and go through a gate. Go across the field and through the gate ahead. Continue through the narrow field to cross a stile on the left. Turn RIGHT along a green track to a road. Now follow this quiet country road LEFT to reach St. Saeran's church in Llanynys.

St Saeran's church, founded in the 6thC, was once the most important church in the area. The present building dating from the 13thC, has an avenue of ancient yee trees leading to an intricately carved Tudor porch. Among its many interesting features are fine hammer beamed roofs, a rare 14thC memorial stone, carved woodwork, and rare telescopic dog tongs used to seize and expel unruly hounds. Undoubtedly its greatest treasure is the large 15thC wall painting of St. Christopher – the patron saint of travellers – discovered in 1967 under plaster. Traditionally his image provided comfort to wayfarers.

2 After visiting the church take a signposted path between the adjoining building (a recently closed inn) and garages, passing in front of cottages to cross a stile into a field, and another one ahead. Continue across the next field to pass just to the left of the second large tree to cross a stream and stile in the boundary ahead. Now head half-RIGHT across the large field to a boundary corner by a wood. Go along the wood edge then follow the stiled path past a house and along a field edge to join its access track. After crossing a bridge over the river cross two stiles on the right to follow the river through three fields to a road. Cross the stile almost opposite and follow the river through five fields to another road. *The red-bricked building on the left is Clwyd Hall, built in 1867-9, for John Taber, a London wine merchant. South of Moel Famau, with its distinctive ruined Jubilee Tower is the shapely hill of Moel Fenlli, and in good light you can make out the ramparts of its Iron-Age fort. Turn RIGHT across the* bridge over the river, then cross a stile on the left. (For the alternative return to Rhewl continue along the road, bear right at the junction, keep ahead at the next to take a signposted path on the left just before cottages. Follow the stiled path through three fields and past the churchyard to Capel Rhewl.)

3 Continue along the riverbank. At the end of the field by a footbridge, turn RIGHT to walk alongside the boundary to pass through a gate into the farmyard of Plas-y-Ward. *This is the seat of one of the Vale's notable families – the Thelwalls – who exercised great local power from the 13thC – 17thC. The current house dates from the 17thC. During the Civil War, Simon Thelwall, a parliamentarian lived here, and Plas-y-Ward featured in accounts of local skirmishes.* Cross the farmyard and bear LEFT between buildings and follow its access drive to the bend of a road. Take the LEFT fork. *To the south is the distinctive spire of St Peter's church, Ruthin.* After a bridge over the course of a former railway line, cross a stile on the right. Now follow a waymarked stiled path through three fields towards Rhewl, and on along Maes Derw to a road. Turn LEFT to reach the A525 then follow it RIGHT back to the Drovers for a drink.

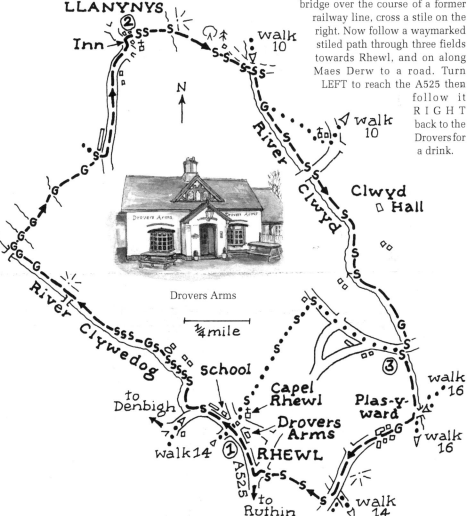

Drovers Arms

¼ mile

AROUND CWM NANT MAWR

DESCRIPTION A 7½ mile (**A**) or 3¾ mile walk (**B**) exploring the attractive rolling hills around the Nant Mawr wooded valley on the western side of the Vale. Quiet country roads linked to a few good paths provide access to a little walked area and enable a return on the final section of the Mynydd Hiraethog trail, featuring a broad ridge at a height of about 800 feet giving panoramic views across the Vale. The walk provides an opportunity to visit St. Dyfnog's Holy Well and Bath and St. Dyfnog's medieval church, containing the famous Jesse window. Allow about 3½ hours. See **Walk 7** for information on the church and Holy Well.

START St. Dyfnog's Church, Llanrhaeadr [SJ 082634]

DIRECTIONS Llanrhaeadr lies just off the A525 Denbigh-Ruthin road.

I After visiting the church, head south along the road out of the village. When it bends towards the A525, continue along the section of old road past the school. At its end cross the A525 with care to the signposted path opposite and follow the stiled path across two fields to a road. Turn LEFT and follow it to a junction. Turn RIGHT along the road, then take a signposted path over a stone stile past the outbuilding of a red-bricked house to turn LEFT along the field edge towards Pentre-Llanrhaeadr. At its end go through a gap, then a kissing gate by houses and on to cross the A525. Take the signposted tarmaced path past the end of the post office up to a small housing estate. Turn RIGHT between the first two houses and follow the enclosed path behind houses to briefly join the pavement, before following a path by a stream to cross a stile into a field.

2 Continue ahead along the field edge, over another stile, then go up the stepped path and on alongside the fence to cross a further stile. Follow the path through the wood to cross a stile into a field. Go half-RIGHT, through a hedge gap, and across the next field to a stile in the far corner. Turn RIGHT up the road. At a junction, turn LEFT. (For **Walk B** continue along the road to point **4**.) Follow the road up past Wern Chapel at a junction, and on up past two further side roads. After a farm, the road rises to a junction. Here, turn RIGHT and follow the road down and up past Ffrith y Ceubren to where the signposted Mynydd Hiraethog trail crosses the road.

3 Cross the stile on the right and follow the waymarked trail along the edge of three fields and across the next – *enjoying extensive views* – to reach a farm's access lane. Go through the right of two gates opposite and follow the boundary on your left to go through the lower of two gates. Turn LEFT up the field edge and through a waymarked gate. Turn RIGHT along the gorse-covered field edge to cross a hidden stile in the corner. Continue ahead to follow a faint green track down the open hillside – *enjoying extensive views* – to cross a stile and another further down at a wood corner. Follow a track down the edge of the wood to join another track coming in from the left. Just after it bends right take a path on the left to cross a waymarked stile below. Follow the path down to reach the bend of a road. Turn RIGHT and follow the road past a house and increasingly extensive woodland.

4 After about ½ mile, at the wood corner and just before a farm, take a signposted path on the left through a small iron gate. Go down a delightful enclosed path at the wood edge, follow a track across the river, then go half-RIGHT on the waymarked path up through trees, later along or just to the right of a sunken section of path. After crossing a stile/sleeper bridge at the top of the wood follow the hedge-lined path up to go through a bridle gate and on to reach a road. Continue ahead and follow the road past cottages and a golf course, later descending to a junction above Bryn Morfydd Hotel. Turn LEFT and follow the road past its entrance driveway and shortly take a signposted path on the right. Follow the path down the edge of the wood, then a field to reach the Vicarage's access lane via a gate. Turn LEFT. After 25 yards, turn RIGHT to pass between gateposts, then go through a gap in the wall on your left. Follow the popular local path down to St. Dynog's Well and Bath, and on down the wooded valley to cross the stream to pass through an arched doorway. Go past the almhouses, through a small gate and on past the pottery and church lychgate.

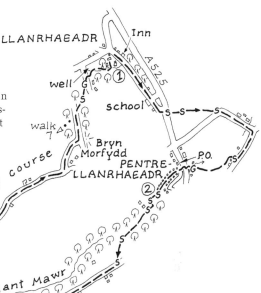

About the author.....

David lives in Denbighshire and has known this part of North Wales for many years, appreciating the beauty and history of its landscape. He is a keen and experienced walker, with an interest in local history and is a member of Denbighshire Local Access Forum. He is also a freelance writer for Walking Wales magazine and has worked as a Rights of Way Surveyor. He hopes that his comprehensive guides will encourage people to explore the countryside's diverse scenery and rich heritage. Visit: www.davidberrywalks.co.uk

WALK 13

AROUND CWM CLEWEDOG

DESCRIPTION A 7½ mile (**A**) or 7 mile (**B**) walk which follows quiet country roads, a section of the Mynnydd Hiraethog trail, and other related linked waymarked paths, to explore the attractive hills adjoining the Clewedog valley, with extensive views. The route rises from the valley near Bontuchel across open slopes, before following the trail down through Coed y Pentre to Cyffylliog, with its medieval church. It climbs a road away from the valley, then follows a choice of higher or lower routes to its northern point. **Walk A** follows a delightful green track up across the open slopes of Moel y Fron, then green lane, with the climbing rewarded with great views. **Walk B** continues on the trail through woodland and farmland (muddy in parts and not recommended after rain) Allow about 4 hours. The route can easily be shortened to 3½ mile (**C**) or 4 mile (**D**) walks using the roads shown.
START Bontuchel [SJ 084578].
DIRECTIONS Bontuchel lies about 2 miles west of Ruthin. Go through the village and just past the bridge over the river is a parking area on the left by a noticeboard.

1 Continue along the road towards Cyffylliog alongside the river past an impressive weir. Just before the road crosses a bridge over the river, go up a side road on the left. After about ¼ mile, just past a farm, turn LEFT up a track to cross a stile. Continue up the track, and immediately after it bends left, take a path on the right, which rises steadily along the edge of the wood to the forestry track. Follow the path opposite up through the conifers to leave the forest by a stile. Continue ahead up the large field, past a solitary tree and on to cross a stile in a fence corner. *Pause to enjoy the extensive view of the Clwydian Hills.* Follow the waymarked path along the edge of three fields and down the middle of the next field to go through a gate. Continue down the field

to reach a lane via a gate. (For **Walk C** turn right down the lane.) Follow it LEFT to go through a gate, where you join the Mynnydd Hiraethog trail. Continue ahead on the signposted tree-lined path down to a gate.

2 About 40 yards further, at a waymarker post, bear RIGHT across the slope to cross a ladder-stile into Coed y Pentre. Follow the path across the wooded slope. Later, after passing along the top wood edge, the path angles down through mainly deciduous trees, then an area of mature conifers, to a stile above the river. Go through the wood and on near the river to a stile by a telephone in Cyffylliog. (For **Walk D** follow the road right.) Turn LEFT to the road junction by the Red Lion. *Along the road almost opposite signposted to Nantglyn is the old Georgian 'hearse house' and medieval Church of St. Mary founded in the 15thC.* Turn RIGHT and follow the road across the river by the school, then at the junction, go up the minor road ahead. The road rises steadily away from the valley passing a small plantation, then a side road.

3 On the bend you have a choice to point 4: **For Walk A,** turn LEFT on the signposted path and follow the green track up across the open slopes of Moel y Fron to eventually reach a road by a cattle-grid. Continue north along the road then take its lower section. Just before the derelict farm, bear RIGHT along an enclosed green lane. After going through a gate, continue on the now open lane – *enjoying extensive views* – soon steadily descending to cross a cattle-grid, where it becomes a fully tarmaced road. A little further you reach where the trail crosses. Continue down the road. **For Walk B** cross a stile in the holly hedge ahead and go along the field edge. Just before the wood, turn RIGHT down to cross a stream and a nearby hidden stile. Continue on the waymarked trail path through the wood and along the bottom edge of two fields. Go past a bungalow and keep ahead down a green track to go through two gates, and along a track behind a farmhouse. After going through a gate by a stream, follow the fence on your right to cross a stile (can be muddy).

Continue ahead near the fence to go through a gate and over a nearby stile. (Here is a short cut to the road.) Continue ahead along the field edge and over a stile in the corner. Keep ahead, then turn LEFT to follow a stony track up through an area of young trees and on to a stile. Go across the field up to a stile onto a road. Turn RIGHT.

4 Follow the road down past Ffrith y Ceubren and up to a junction. Turn RIGHT. When the road splits, go down the right fork and follow it past a farm and a bungalow to cross a stile on the left opposite an access track. Follow the field

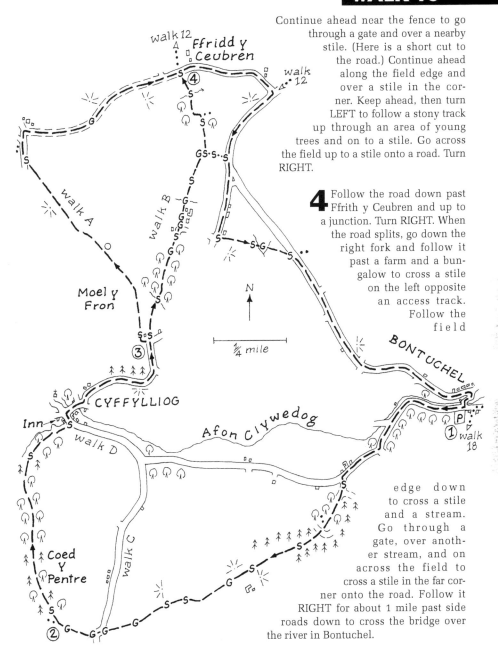

edge down to cross a stile and a stream. Go through a gate, over another stream, and on across the field to cross a stile in the far corner onto the road. Follow it RIGHT for about 1 mile past side roads down to cross the bridge over the river in Bontuchel.

WALK 14

LADY BAGOT'S DRIVE

DESCRIPTION The wooded Clywedog valley, with its delightful limestone river scenery, offers one of the Vale's finest walks. The whole valley can be included in a delightful waymarked 4 mile circuit (**C**) from Rhewl - a favourite short walk of mine. The full described route goes from Ruthin via the medieval church at Llanfwrog to the Clywedog valley, and offers either a 7 mile (**A**) or a 4½ mile (**B**) walk, returning from Rhewl via field paths. [Please note that the final riverside section will not be accessible until the current construction of a new Ruthin north link road and bridge is completed in August 2006.] Allow about 4 hours for the long walk. The popular Drovers Arms at Rhewl (01824 703163), with its traditional ales and good daily food, makes a fine ending or mid-way break.

START Crispin Yard car park, Ruthin [SJ 121582] or the Drovers Arms, Rhewl [SJ 109604].

DIRECTIONS For the Ruthin start see **Walk 17**. For the Rhewl start see **Walk 11**.

The route along the Clywedog valley follows an old coach drive, known locally as Lady Bagot's Drive, which ran from Rhewl through the Pool Park estate once owned by the Bagot family. It was also part of a proposed narrow gauge railway from Ruthin to Cerrigydrudion, work on which started in 1879, but was abandoned in 1884.

For **Walk C**, from the Drovers Arms go to the nearby road signposted to Llanynys, then cross the A525 to the lane almost opposite to join a path signposted to Bontuchel. Cross the bridge and follow the lane, soon becoming a track, alongside the river, past a former mill, a leat which provided it with water, and old limekilns to join the main walk at Tyn y coed in the wooded river valley at point 3. Follow the directions in paragraphs 3 and 4 to complete the valley walk circuit and return to Rhewl.

Walks A and B

1 From the Ruthin car park entrance, turn LEFT over the river and at the junction continue ahead up Mwrog Street, then on the B5105 (Cerrigydrudion) through Llanfwrog to go up steps to the Church of St. Mwrog. *The late medieval church stands on a small hill within a circular Celtic churchyard.* Return down the steps, then follow a path LEFT between houses to cross a stile and footbridge. Turn LEFT to cross a stone stile in the corner. Turn RIGHT, cross a stile, then head down the field towards houses to cross a wooden stile near garages Follow the field boundary past a playground and houses to another stile, then go along an enclosed path behind houses, then on across a section of field to a stile.

2 Continue up the field edge to cross a stile in the top corner. Follow the path along the edge of three fields to a farm lane. Cross the stile opposite and go along the field edge past a farm, then follow the waymarked stiled path through further fields to a lane. Turn LEFT, then RIGHT down a track then follow a path past the side of a house and on down to cross a footbridge over the river Clywedog to reach a track by Tyn y Coed in the wooded Clywedog valley. (For **Walk B**, turn right and follow the track alongside the river, past old limekilns, and a leat which diverted water to power a former mill which you later pass, and on with a lane to cross the river to the A525 at Rhewl to resume the main route at point **5**.) For **Walk A** turn LEFT.

3 Continue up the valley alongside the river on the former Lady Bagot's Drive. *In spring, the wood is full of bluebells and wild garlic. The river tumbles over a series of rock strata.* Go past a footbridge, and later, at a finger post, turn RIGHT to follow a waymarked path rising steadily through the wood. Cross a stile and go across a field to re-enter the wood. Follow the path, keeping ahead at a signposted path junction, to eventually cross a stile into a field. *Ahead is a panoramic view of the Clwydian Hills.*

Bontuchel

4 Go over the stiles ahead, then follow a waymarked path through the edge of the next five fields, then after a corrugated barn turn RIGHT to follow a track alongside a wood to cross a stile. Continue through the wood to join and follow a driveway to the A525. Turn RIGHT and proceed WITH CAUTION along the road into Rhewl. *The Welsh poem inscribed on the bridge is reputed to be by the bard Twm o'r Nant. Tradition has it that a battle fought here during the Civil War made the river run with blood. Rhewl was the home of Emyrs Ap Iwan – a famous Welsh Methodist minister and bard. The Drovers Arms was an important stop for drovers and makes a good refreshment stop now. It is said to be haunted – just ask the landlord!*

(An alternative riverside route via Plas-y-Ward is shown). Cross the stile opposite and turn LEFT to cross a stile near the stone road bridge. Turn RIGHT and walk alongside the fence to go through a gate. Continue ahead across a wide bridge over the stream and through another gate. Head half-RIGHT to cross a stile in the fence. Go along the field edge, over another stile, then continue ahead across two further fields to reach the new Ruthin northern link road. Follow the diverted path to the nearby river Clwyd, pass under the road bridge then continue south alongside the river towards Ruthin. Later cross a footbridge over the river and follow the path to the road. Follow it RIGHT back to the start.

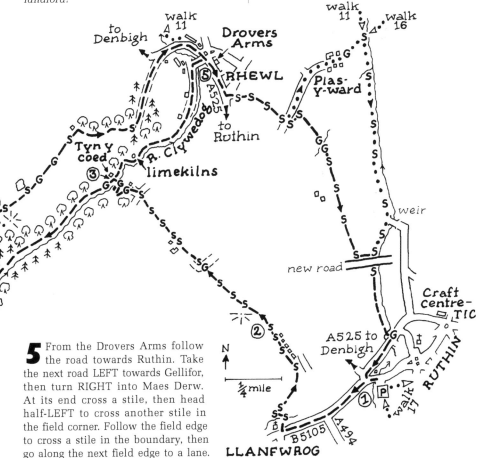

5 From the Drovers Arms follow the road towards Ruthin. Take the next road LEFT towards Gellifor, then turn RIGHT into Maes Derw. At its end cross a stile, then head half-LEFT to cross another stile in the field corner. Follow the field edge to cross a stile in the boundary, then go along the next field edge to a lane.

ST PETER'S CHURCH

DESCRIPTION A 3½ mile walk between Ruthin and Llanbedr Dyffryn-Clwyd, featuring the interesting medieval church of St Peter on open slopes, its Victorian replacement, a country inn and good views. Allow about 2 hours.
START Ruthin Craft Centre/Tourist Information Centre [SJ 126586].
DIRECTIONS The Craft Centre lies on the ring road. There is a car park opposite.

I From the nearby roundabout take the A494 Mold road. When it bends right, turn LEFT along Greenfield Road and follow it past houses and into open country. On the bend by a house, cross a stile ahead then follow a hedge-lined track down to cross a bridge. Shortly leave the track by a stile on the left. Turn RIGHT and follow the stiled path through two fields to a track. Cross a stile opposite and go up the field edge to a stile then follow the enclosed path to the B5429.

2 Turn RIGHT along the road. Just past a housing estate turn LEFT on a signposted path up Llanbedr Hall's driveway. Shortly, take the path up to the medieval St Peter's church. *It contains the grave of Joseph Ablett, who lived at nearby Llanbedr Hall in the 19thC, and who generously donated land for the building of the North Wales Hospital in Denbigh.* Return to the B5429 and follow it through Llanbedr Dyffryn-Clwyd to the A494 by the Griffin Inn. *The nearby Victorian church of St Peter contains an elaborately carved stone in the porch – part of a 14th C gravestone found in the old church site to the north.*

3 Turn RIGHT towards Ruthin and just before a bus shelter take a signposted path through a gate. Go down the large field past a tree to a stile in the bottom corner, and across the next field to cross a stile onto a lane. Go through the small gate opposite and follow the boundary on your right down to cross a stile/footbridge. Turn LEFT to cross a larger footbridge and go along the field edge, over a stile, across the next field and a farm driveway. Angle up the field to a stile in the top corner by Ruthin School. Go past the back of the school buildings, then turn RIGHT to follow the road past houses, soon descending to join your outward route.

COED CEUNANT

DESCRIPTION A delightfully varied 7½ mile walk across the Vale to the lower slopes of the Clwydian Hills, featuring attractive woodland, old bridleways and a fine riverside finish. Allow about 4 hours.
START As **Walk 15**.

I Follow instructions in section **1** of **Walk 15** to the B5429.

2 Go along the road opposite past a school. At Pen-y-Waen, turn RIGHT along a green hedge-lined track, soon bending right. 75 yards after it bends left cross a stile on the right. Go across the field to cross a stream and stile. Go up the next field, through a gate in the fence and continue in the same direction up to cross a stile in the top field corner. Turn LEFT up the gated Llanbedr Hall driveway past entrances to Longwater. Just after crossing a cattle grid, go through a kissing gate on the left and follow the rising green track to enter Coed Ceunant, owned by the Woodland Trust. Follow it through the wood then take a path which passes below a cottage to go through a kissing gate to reach a small pool. *This is the highest point of the walk.*

3 Turn LEFT past the end of the pool, then descend LEFT to go through another kissing gate. Follow the path along the top edge of the deep wooded valley, descending through a small clearing to go through a kissing gate by the stream. Turn RIGHT up a track, go through a gate and along the field edge to cross a stile. Turn LEFT and follow the boundary through two gates. Cross a stream and continue across the field to go through gate in a corner fence by a green cross-track. Continue between a line of trees and a fence, through a gate, and on above gorse to cross a stile.

(Map labels:)

Fron Goch
HIRWAEN
Moel y Gaer
walk 11
Clyttir
WALK 16
N
¼ mile
Melin y wern
walk 11
school
St Peter's Church
Coed Ceunant
Llanbedr Hall
LLANBEDR DYFFRYN-CLWYD
weir
WALK 15
Inn
Craft Centre TIC
new road
School
RUTHIN
A494 to Mold

4 Go down a green track into an attractiveside valley. *Above is Moel-y-Gaer – an isolated iron-age hillfort.* At a waymarker post turn LEFT down to cross a stile. Continue ahead down to cross a footbridge and a nearby stile. Go past a cottage, then take the waymarked path up the right fork of an access track. Shortly after a cattle grid, when the track angles down, keep ahead on the waymarked path. Just before a stile above Fron Goch, turn LEFT down to cross a stile in the fence below. (This is a local diversion of a RoW through Fron Goch. Look out for any signs indicating a formal diversion route change) Rejoin the access track and follow it to the road at Hirwaen. Go down the enclosed bridleway opposite and along a road. After 50 yards, go along a track to Greystones, and continue along a delightful hedge-lined sunken sandstone bridleway.Go past Tyn-y-

Celyn and continue on the enclosed gated bridleway and on through Clyttir farmyard to a road. Follow another enclosed bridleway opposite, then turn RIGHT along a road.

5 Shortly, turn LEFT along the access track to Melin y Wern. (to extend the riverside walking take a signposted path from Minffordd as indicated.) Follow the track past an old watermill, over a stream and on to cross a footbridge over the river Clwyd. Turn LEFT and follow the stiled riverside path through several fields, past the sewage works, a weir and on alternative road return. Continue with the riverside path passing under a new road bridge to eventually cross a footbridge over the river to reach the nearby main road via a kissing gate. Turn LEFT to return to the start.

14thC gravestone, St Peter's Church Llanbedr Dyffryn-Clwyd

WALK 17
RUTHIN TO EYARTH HALT

DESCRIPTION A fascinating 5½-mile walk (**A**) exploring part of Ruthin's historical centre and the countryside south of the town. The route passes many places of interest, including medieval churches, old houses, ancient earthworks, a former railway station, and a country pub at Llanfair. Allow about 3 hours, with extra time for sightseeing. The route can easily be shortened to a 4 mile walk (**B**) as shown.
START Crispin Yard car park, Ruthin [SJ 121582] or alternatively Ruthin Craft Centre [SJ 126586].
DIRECTIONS The car park with toilets is at the bottom of Clwyd Street just past Ruthin Gaol on the western side of Ruthin.

1 Take a path leading from the toilets to pass the end of houses. Turn RIGHT then take a path rising beneath a castellated wall and follow it up to the road by Ruthin Castle entrance. Turn LEFT, shortly passing Nant Clwyd House – *a 14thC timber-framed hall house* – to reach St Peter's Square. *The Old Court House (National Westminster Bank) was built in 1401 as the local administrative centre, court and jail. In front of Barclays Bank is 'Maen Huail' – an early medieval stone, traditionally used by King Arthur to behead a love-rival. Next to the imposing Georgian Castle Hotel is the 17thC Myddelton Arms, with its triple tier of dormer windows. Nearby is St Peter's Church, founded in 1310. Its distinctive spire – the only one in the Vale – is a Victorian addition. The church has elaborately decorated 16thC timber roofs, and rare monumental brasses. Behind the church are the 14thC Old Cloister, the 18thC Grammar School, and old almshouses.* From the square head down Market Street to the Craft Centre.

2 Take the A494 Mold road, and when the road swings right go ahead up Bryn Goodman, then turn RIGHT along the drive of Ruthin School. *Founded as a grammar school in 1574 by Dr. Gabriel, it moved to its present site in 1889.* At the A494 follow it LEFT out of Ruthin to the entrance to Caer Groes Farm. Cross the road and a stile opposite by Hafod. Go ahead through two fields, then through a facing gate part-way along a third field and follow a farm track to a road. Before going along the track opposite follow the road LEFT to visit the 15thC St. Meugan's church. *It contains fine memorial stones, and a rare ornate 17thC altar. Outside stands a medieval preaching cross.* Retrace your steps to follow the track to a farm. Go past outbuildings and when opposite the near end of the farmhouse go through a small waymarked gate, passing between other buildings to reach a road.

3 Go through the gate opposite and along the field edge to pass through a gate. *There are fine views of the nearby Clwydian Hills.* Continue across the next field to cross a stile by two gates. Follow the boundary on your left through two further fields. After a stile, turn LEFT (or right for **Walk B**) along the field edge to reach a road. Follow it LEFT. On the bend go ahead along an access track past the lodge and later Plas Newydd Farm to eventually reach a road. Turn RIGHT – *enjoying good views of 17thC Plas Newydd, and to the south the limestone crags above Graigfechan, and the prominent 17thC house of Garth Gynan.* Follow the road into Llanfair D.C., then turn RIGHT along the A525. *In this compact village centre is the 15thC church of St. Mary and St. Cynfarch, with many interesting features and worth a visit.*

4 Go past the White Horse Inn and the village hall out of the village. Shortly, take a signposted path on the left. Follow the path along field edges down to a road. *Opposite is the former Eyarth railway station, an intermediate halt on the Ruthin to Corwen branch line, which opened in 1864. Now a country guest house, it retains the ticket office and platform. The station dealt mainly with agricultural produce, livestock and domestic coal. Passenger services ended in 1953 and the line finally closed in 1962.* Turn RIGHT, then take a signposted path on the left past its boundary to cross a ladder-stile into a large field. Head half-RIGHT to cross a stile by a water trough. Go ahead across two further fields to enter a third below Ffynogion Farm – *an early 16thC timber-framed house. One of its most colourful owners (1872-1908) was Sir John Puleston. Educated at Ruthin School, he sought his fortune in America, becoming an editor, lawyer, banker, and friend of Abraham Lincoln, and on his return, treasurer of the National Eisteddfod Association.* Follow the boundary on the left past a partly hidden pond – *ahead is the low embankment of a medieval moated homestead – a scheduled monument* – to go through a gate. Go across the field, through another gate and on towards the farm to pass round its right hand side to go through a gate. Continue along its access lane. Immediately after crossing the river, go over a stile on the right. Now head half-LEFT to the far field corner to go through two gates onto the road. Follow it RIGHT for $^1/_3$ mile.

5 Cross a stile by the entrance to Scott House – *built as a nurses' home in 1933.* Go along the field edge, and just before a stone bridge over the river, go through a kissing-gate, then a short tunnel. Continue through the riverside meadow and park to your starting point. *Up on your right is Ruthin Castle Hotel, built in 1853 on the site of a castle started by Edward I in 1277 and demolished in 1646 by Parliamentary forces during the Civil War.*

COED Y FRON-WYLLT

DESCRIPTION An easy 2¼ mile (**A**) or 1½ mile (**B**) walk exploring the attractive mixed woodland of Coed y Fron-wyllt in the Nant Melin-dwr valley, and an opportunity to visit a bird hide. Allow about 1½ hours.
START Forest car park, near Bontuchel [SJ 082571].
DIRECTIONS From Bontuchel, take the road signposted to Clocaenog to find the forest track leading to the signposted car park on the left after nearly ½ mile.

1 After visiting the signposted hide overlooking small pools in the wooded valley alongside the river, return to the track and follow it down into the wooded valley, soon crossing the river and rising to join another track. Turn sharp RIGHT and follow the track above the river. After a large turning area where the track splits, continue along the stony track rising gently towards a distant white house with more open views.

2 After about 200 yards, take a path angling back on the left. Follow the former forestry track, now a delightful path through the deciduous woodland to join a narrow forestry track (a bridleway). It gently descends,

BONTUCHEL

walk 13

Coed y Fron-wyllt

hide

N

¼ mile

soon joining a wider forestry track, which takes you past a large house, part of which dates from 1600, and on to reach a track junction. (For **Walk B**, turn sharp LEFT to follow the track above the wooded valley to join your outward route.)

3 For **Walk A** continue ahead on the track past cottages to take a narrow path angling down to the road. Turn LEFT and follow the road into Bontuchel. Turn LEFT along the road signposted to Clocaenog. Shortly, at the entrance to Ty-Brith, take a path on the left angling down to cross a footbridge over the river. Follow the path up across the wooded slope to a track. Follow it RIGHT to the track junction, taking the right fork back to the start.

COED CIL-Y-GROESLWYD & EFENECHTYD

DESCRIPTION A 4 mile walk exploring the undulating countryside around the Vale of Efenechtyd. The walk features a short circuit (optional) of Coed Cil-y-groeslwyd Nature Reserve, an ancient ash/yew woodland on a limestone ridge, a delightful 13th C church in the ancient hamlet of Efenechtyd, Pen-y-Gaer Iron Age hillfort, accessed by an old green lane (muddy in parts during winter) and good views. Allow about 3 hours. The route can easily be shortened and Coed Cil-y-groeslwyd accessed by a footpath from near Pont Eyarth a shown.
START Village Hall, Pwll-glas [SJ 118548].
DIRECTIONS Pwll-glas lies on the A494 south of Ruthin. The walk starts from the telephone/bus shelter near the village hall. Nearby parking alongside the grass verge.

1 Go along to the nearby minor road past Capel y Rhiw. Follow the road up to a junction and take the lane opposite. Follow the wooded lane past houses and at its end continue ahead to cross a stile by a finger post. (If not wishing to visit Coed Cil-y-

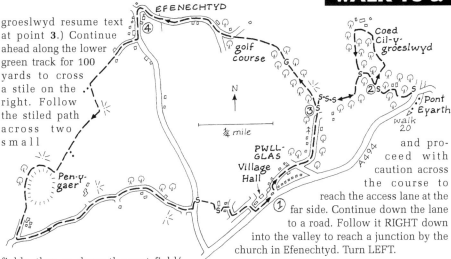

groeslwyd resume text at point **3**.) Continue ahead along the lower green track for 100 yards to cross a stile on the right. Follow the stiled path across two small

and proceed with caution across the course to reach the access lane at the far side. Continue down the lane to a road. Follow it RIGHT down into the valley to reach a junction by the church in Efenechtyd. Turn LEFT.

fields, then go down the next field/ wood edge. Just before a small limestone ridge, turn LEFT for 30 yards, then go half-RIGHT upon the ridge and on to cross a large ladder-stile ahead to enter Coed Cil-y-groeslwyd (the wood of the grey cross) Nature Reserve. *Managed by North Wales Wildlife Trust and an SSSI, it provides a habitat for a diversity of plants, birds, animals and butterflies. Follow the path through the wood to an information board.* Do a U-turn to pass behind the board.

2 Follow the path alongside the boundary fence on a gentle descent to the edge of the wood. Here turn LEFT to follow the path alongside the old wall, enjoying occasional views of the Clwydian Hills. After crossing a leaning tree, just before farm buildings at the wood corner, turn LEFT. After a few yards, bear RIGHT across the remains of an old quarry, then follow a path along the wood edge past the farm, briefly rising, before bending LEFT to run alongside the fence boundary of the wood to reach the large ladder-stile. Retrace your steps to the stile near the lane end.

3 Take the signposted path up the green track – *soon enjoying good views of the Clwydians*. Follow the path across the open gorse/tree covered limestone slope to go through a small wooden gate. Follow the path to the golf course. Heed the warnings

The small 13th church of St. Michael and All Angels reputedly stands on the site of an earlier Celtic church or 'llan', possibly founded by monks from St. Saeran's community at Llanynys , on an intersection of ancient highways near the Pilgrims route from Holywell to S. Davids. St. Michael was once the patron saint of travellers. Its many interesting features include 16th C roof timbers and a rare medieval wooden font.

4 After visiting the church continue along the road past 18th C Plas-yn-llan. Just past large outbuildings, turn RIGHT up the lane past Pen-y-Bryn, after which this former road becomes a green track. At a facing gate, when the track splits, bear LEFT up a short narrow section of the hedge-lined track to a viewpoint When the track splits again, keep ahead to follow the track round the site of Pen-y-Gaer hillfort, after which it descends to pass a farm to reach a road. Turn LEFT and follow the road down into the Vale of Efenechtyd – *enjoying good views*. At a junction, turn LEFT then take the signposted path on the right over a stile. Follow the boundary on your left down and past a house to cross a stile. Go through a gap in the hedge opposite and follow a path down to pass between houses. Turn RIGHT down the road, soon bending LEFT. Shortly, turn RIGHT to the A494. Follow the pavement LEFT back to the start.

CRAIG ADWY-WYNT & NANTCLWYD HALL

DESCRIPTION A 7½ mile walk (**A**) exploring the delightful varied countryside south of Llanfair Dyffryn Clwyd. Highlights include a wooded gorge, limestone crags, open parkland, 17thC Nantclwyd Hall, lakes, woodland, a 15thC house, old bridleways, and good views. Allow about 4½ hours. The route can easily be shortened to a 3½ mile walk (**B**).

START Llanfair Dyffryn Clwyd [SJ134554] or alternatively Pont Eyarth [SJ 127553].

DIRECTIONS From Ruthin take the A525 towards Wrexham to reach Llanfair Dyffryn Clwyd after about 2 miles. Parking is limited in the centre. For the alternative start, turn right in the village towards Pwll-glas, and park on the right just after an old railway bridge. (Please do not block the gateway.)

From Llanfair follow the road signposted to Pwll-glas to reach the A494. Here go through a kissing gate on the left and along a delightful wooded gorge above the river Clwyd, on the trackbed of the former Denbigh-Corwen railway. After passing a ruin into a small clearing by two houses, the path bears LEFT up through the trees, then crosses the part-wooded slope between fences. At the fence corner, turn LEFT up to cross a stile and head up the field to cross two stiles below a house. Follow a path behind the house and up alongside a fence to the end of a wall.

2 Here, the path bears RIGHT up past a side path (which leads to the site of a narrow iron-age hillfort), and continues through an attractive area of gorse, heather and small trees to eventually reach a gate near derelict buildings. (For **Walk B**, go through the gate and down between the buildings to follow a waymarked path meandering through the wood, then down its edge and a field to a road. Follow it right to resume the main walk at point **6**.) For **Walk A** continue RIGHT up the path to go through a gate. Follow the path RIGHT through a more open bracken-covered area, to reach the shrub-covered limestone ridge of Craig-Adwy-wynt. Continue along the ridge, enjoying the extensive views. After the second of two old fences, gently descend the green end of the ridge to follow a path through bracken, soon bending south through further bracken to cross a stile in the fence corner. Now head almost half-RIGHT across rough pasture to cross a stile hidden behind the left-hand side of a large corrugated barn into Coppice Wood. Follow a path past a ruined cottage and an outbuilding and on through the wood to leave it by a waymarked gate.

3 Continue ahead across the field. At a gate in the far boundary, turn RIGHT down a green track and through a gate. When it swings right, go through a gate ahead, and down through the wood, soon bearing half-RIGHT to leave the wood by a small gate. Continue just beneath the wood boundary for about 120 yards, then gradually angle away down towards distant Nantclwyd Hall and its lake. Pass just above the corner of a small wood and go down a faint green track, then head towards a windsock to cross a stream just beyond, to go through a gate. *The current hall dating from the 17thC, was extended in Victorian times, then remodelled, and the grounds enhanced from the mid 1950s by the eminent Welsh architect Sir Clough William-Ellis, of Portmeirion fame. It has been owned by the Naylor-Leyland family since the early 19thC. Nantclwyd is known as the birthplace of lawn tennis, for it was on the croquet lawn, during a visit in 1873, that Major Walter Clopton Wingfield, its inventor, played the first game.* Continue ahead to cross the river Clwyd by a delightful wooden bridge. Turn LEFT along the river bank and go through a gate to cross the driveway. Continue ahead to pass a former road bridge over the river to reach the A494. Turn LEFT along the verge, then take the next road LEFT (Llanelidan). Now follow the road signposted to Graigadwywynt past a lodge then a gateway to the hall guarded by majestic stone eagles. Continue along the road.

4 After another similar gateway, take a signposted path through a gate on the right and on over a stile. Continue past Sawmill Pool and a small wood, then follow a green track across pastureland to go through a gate. Immediately do a U-turn into the adjoining field and head half-RIGHT up to go through an old gateway in the tree boundary. Follow a track by the stream up to a road. Continue ahead along the road and at a junction turn RIGHT. When the road bends right, go along the access track to Ffynnon y Milgi to cross a stile just ahead on your left. (An earlier stile offers an alternative linked path)

5 Go ahead along the field edge, through an old gateway in the corner, and on to cross a stile in the next field corner. Follow a path, with the fence on your left, along the bottom edge of a tree-covered limestone ridge to cross two stiles into a field. Follow the stiled path along the edge of three large fields to enter a wood. Head half-LEFT through the trees, over a stile and along a field edge to a road. Follow it RIGHT, and at the junction, turn RIGHT. Shortly turn LEFT down the access track to Plas Uchaf – *a late 15thC hall house, containing important 16thC wall paintings, said to have once included a courthouse and prison.* When it bends right to the house continue ahead on another track to eventually reach a road. Follow it RIGHT.

6 Shortly, turn RIGHT along an access track (a bridleway) to pass Pistyll Gwyn. Continue down the track, through a small wood and on to pass the front of Garreg Bach. Go between the garden wall and a fence, through a bridle gate and on to cross a footbridge over Afon Hesbin. Now follow the hedge-lined bridleway, then an access track, back to Llanfair D.C.

35

AFON Y MAES VALLEY

DESCRIPTION This splendid, figure of eight, 7 mile walk explores the beautiful unspoilt undulating countryside of the Nantclwyd estate around Llanelidan, situated in the narrower upper part of the Vale, enclosed by hills. Highlights include a medieval church, Nantclwyd Hall, delightful old bridleways, and excellent views. Allow about 4 hours. The walk can easily be undertaken in various shorter permutations ranging from 2 – 5 miles.

START Llanelidan [SJ 108503].

DIRECTIONS From Ruthin take the A494 towards Bala. 2 miles after Pwllglas, turn left towards Llanelidan. Keep ahead at a cross-roads as you enter the village, then go down a 'No through road' past houses, telephone, and a chapel to its end and a parking area.

1 Go past nearby Rose Cottage, over a stile and follow the stream to a road. Follow it RIGHT, passing the Leyland Arms (1844), to reach the 15thC St Eliden's church. *Dedicated to an obscure local saint, it has a long association with nearby Nantclwyd Hall. It retains many medieval features, including fine carved wood work.* After visiting the church, continue along the road and just past Lletty Cottage, cross a stile on the left. Follow a green track, through a gate and on across pastureland to reach a road by Sawmill Pool. Turn LEFT to pass an imposing side entrance of Nantclwyd Hall, guarded by magnificent stone eagles. For a good view of the Hall dating from the 17thC continue along the road for about 150 yards. *For more information on the Hall refer to* **Walk 13**. Retrace your steps, then turn sharp RIGHT to go beneath a weeping willow to cross a stile into a field.

2 Head half-LEFT, to pass along the right edge of a small wooded knoll and on over two stiles to the road by Garth-y-neuadd. Follow it LEFT up past a junction, then cross a stile on the left. Go diagonally down the steep field, aiming to the right of the distant cricket pavilion, to cross a stile and stone footbridge. Head half-RIGHT, over a stile in the wooden fence, and on past the cricket pavilion to the road. Follow your outward path back to the start.

3 At the far end of the parking area turn RIGHT along an enclosed path to cross a stile on the left. Continue ahead down the field, over a stone footbridge and a stile. Now follow the boundary on your left up the field, and just before a gate, turn RIGHT to pass beneath a farm. About 100 yards beyond outbuildings, head half-RIGHT down the slope – *with good views looking down the Vale* – to cross a stile and a footbridge near the field/wood corner. Go across the next field to a gate onto a lane by a house. Go through the gate opposite and continue ahead across four fields through gates, over a stile and across the mid-slope of the next field to walk below a wood. Cross a stile in the wood boundary, turn RIGHT and continue through this attractive mixed woodland, soon just above the stream to cross a stile into a field. Continue near the stream to go through a gate to join a crossing bridleway in a small wooded dingle. (The walk can be shortened here by turning sharp right over the stream, through another gate, and following the bridleway to point **6**.)

4 Continue up the bridleway through two gates to a road. Follow it LEFT – *enjoying extensive views of Clocaenog Forest, the Vale of Clwyd, and the Clwydian Hills.* Shortly, turn RIGHT to follow another gated tree-lined bridleway, later providing views of the Llantisilio Mountains and Moel Ferna as it passes a stile and begins to descend. At the end of the tree-lined section go through a gate on the left and follow the fence on your right round to join and follow a faint green track to go through a bridle gate. Continue ahead on a track to Gwrych-bedw. Go through the farmyard and past the farmhouse. At the stone barn beyond go through the LEFT of two facing gates. Head nearly half-LEFT, soon descending to pass about 25 yards above a large tree to join a path by an old fence post, at the end of a small wooded valley, to cross a stream and on through a gate.

5 Continue up the slope ahead and across the field to go through a gate in the left-hand corner. Go up the field, through a gate by Cwm farmhouse and follow its access track to a road. Turn RIGHT and follow the road for about a mile. *This attractive quiet country road offers extensive views, especially of the Llantisilio Mountains, the Dee Valley and the Berwyn Mountains beyond.* At a junction turn RIGHT. Follow this road down past a house, then turn LEFT along a signposted tree-lined bridleway. At a field, the bridleway continues RIGHT, round the field edge passing two gates, to go through a bridle gate, then resumes its tree-lined character on a long gentle descent, later becoming more of a sunken green lane, to eventually go through a bridle gate at a stream to join a track. Turn LEFT.

6 Continue up the track, past a house, along its access lane, then turn RIGHT along a road. Shortly, cross a stile on your right opposite a large stone building. Head half-LEFT to cross a hidden stile in the field corner. Turn LEFT, and follow the edge of two fields to pass through a facing gate. Follow the boundary on your right and go through a gateway in it, just past a house. Now follow the boundary on your left down to cross a stile and go down through the wood to a road. Turn RIGHT, then shortly, take a signposted path on the left through attractive woodland back to the start.

ON THE PILGRIMS' TRAIL

DESCRIPTION This delightful 6¼ mile walk explores a little known area at the southern end of the Vale of Clwyd. It visits two remote hamlets set in a deep valley on an ancient Pilgrims' track. The undulating route follows riverside and field paths, tracks, bridleways and quiet lanes through attractive wooded valleys, and includes a visit to a medieval country church. Allow about 3½ hours. The route includes an optional extension to visit another medieval church at Derwen, adding 2 miles to the walk, or can be undertaken as two shorter circuits of 4 and 3½ miles using the link road shown.

START Melin-y-Weg [SJ 487040] or alternatively Bettws Gwerfil Goch [SJ 466033]

DIRECTIONS From Ruthin take the B5105 towards Cerrigydridion, then at Clawdd-newyd take the road to Melin-y-Weg. *This quiet road is part of an ancient route used by medieval pilgrims travelling between St Winifred's Well at Holywell to St David's Cathedral in Pembrokeshire. About ½ mile after passing a turn to Derwen look for the gated stone wall surrounding Ffynnon Sarah Well on the right by the entrance to Braich Farm. A visit to this remote medieval holy well is recommended. The tree-shaded stone bath filled by a spring, which was used well into the 19thC, was reputed to heal rheumatism and cancer. It was a custom for sufferers to drop in pins before starting their bathe. Continue along the road to descend to a cross-road in Melin-y-Weg. Park by a notice board or go up the road opposite to park on the bend by a footpath sign. For the alternative start, continue to Bettws Gwerfil Goch to park by the church.*

1 From the cross-road take the road towards Bettws Gwerfil Goch. Just past a chapel turn LEFT along a driveway, then follow a signposted path on the right alongside the infant River Clwyd to reach a track by a farm. Follow it LEFT to pass in front of Glanrafon and cross a footbridge over the river. Turn RIGHT to follow the river to cross a stile, and continue on the riverside path through the wooded valley to eventually cross a stile. *You may well see herons fishing in the river.* Continue on the riverside path, past a stile and on alongside the fence to cross a stile in a facing fence. The path rises gently to another stile. Go half-LEFT up to the bend of a green track. Follow it down then go across the meadow to cross a stile just above the river. Go through the next two fields and past a farmhouse dated 1774. Follow its access track along the valley. (To extend the walk to Derwen to visit the church of St Mary and its 15thC preaching cross in the churchyard – one of the finest in Wales – follow the track to its end and continue along a lane into the village. Simply retrace your steps to resume the main walk.)

2 About 200 yards after passing Tyn-y-coed cottage, as the track begins to rise, go down an enclosed sunken path on your right. The path descends to cross a footbridge over the river, then rises through trees to a track by an old

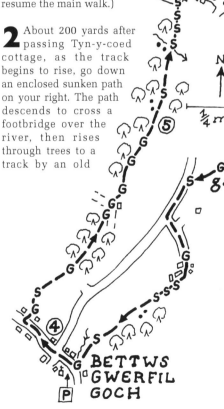

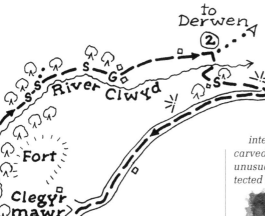

open woodland, and across a field to reach the road in Bettws Gwerfil Goch. Follow it RIGHT to the church. *St Mary's church was founded in the 12thC for pilgrims by Princess Gwerfil of Meironydd, the red-haired granddaughter of King Owain Gwynedd of North Wales. Rebuilt in the 15thC, it contains many interesting features, notably unique 15thC carved panels, a fine carved roof, and an unusual chandelier. It is also home to a protected colony of bats. A key is available.*

Ffynnon Sarah Well

house. Follow it LEFT up to a road. Turn RIGHT and follow this quiet country road for nearly a mile to the entrance to Clegyr Mawr – *behind which is the site of an Iron-Age hillfort.* Continue up the road. (To shorten the walk simply follow the road down to Melin-y-Wig.)

3 Shortly, turn LEFT to follow a signposted path down a lane, then RIGHT along the track to Bryn-halen mawr. Pass just to the right of two outbuildings, through a gate and along a green track (a bridleway) After a gate the bridleway crosses the hillside to join a track. Turn RIGHT. *There are fine views ahead of the Arans, and Cader Idris.* Follow the track to a farm and go through several gates to pass the left-hand side of outbuildings to enter a field. Follow the boundary on your right past a gate to go through another in the bottom corner, then head down the field to a stile onto the road. Follow it LEFT, then take a signposted path LEFT up an access lane, keeping ahead when it splits to reach a farm. Here, turn RIGHT between the farmhouse and outbuildings, then go half-LEFT across the farmyard to a gate then ladder-stile at the end of a long barn. Follow the waymarked stiled path along the bottom edge of two fields and

4 At the cross-road continue up the road ahead, and just past the school turn RIGHT on a signposted path. Go through a gate, then follow the boundary on the left round to cross a stile. Head half-RIGHT to cross the slope of the next field to go through a gate in the far bottom corner. The path now passes through attractive woodland, then two gates by a farm. Continue ahead on a delightful gated track skirting the edge of mature woodland. *Look out for buzzards.*

5 As the track begins to rise left, keep straight ahead on a path through trees and over a field to cross a ladder-stile. Continue ahead alongside an irregular hedge/tree boundary on your right to go into the adjoining field just before a facing wall. Continue ahead and when a faint green track rises half-left, keep ahead to cross a sleeper-bridge and ladder-stile. Follow the wall on your right to cross a stone stile in the corner. Continue ahead across a wettish reedy field, over a stile and a footbridge, and on to reach the road at the alternative parking area in Melin-y-Weg.

PRONUNCIATION

These basic points should help non-Welsh speakers

Welsh	English equivalent
c	always hard, as in 'cat'
ch	as on the Scottish word 'lo**ch**'
dd	as th in '**then**'
f	as f in of
ff	as **ff** in o**ff**
g	always hard as in 'got'
ll	no real equivalent. It is like 'th' in **then**, but with an 'L' sound added to it, giving '**thlan**' for the pronunciation of the Welsh 'Llan'.

In Welsh the accent usually falls on the last-but-one syllable of a word.

KEY TO THE MAPS

- ➙ Walk route and direction
- ═══ Metalled road
- ─ ─ ─ Unsurfaced road
- •••• Footpath/route adjoining walk route
- ⌇⌇⤳ River/stream
- ⋔♋ Trees
- ▬▭ Railway
- **G** Gate
- **S** Stile
- F.B. Footbridge
- ⌄⌄ Viewpoint
- P Parking
- T Telephone

THE COUNTRYSIDE CODE

- Be safe – plan ahead and follow any signs
- Leave gates and property as you find them
- Protect plants and animals, and take your litter home
- Keep dogs under close control
- Consider other people

Some routes cross land where walkers have a legal right of access under the CRoW Act 2000, introduced in May 2005. Open Access land is detailed on OS Explorer maps OL18, OL 23 and 255 which cover this area. This access can be subject to restrictions and closure for land management or safety reasons for up to 28 days a year. Please respect any notices. The Countryside Council for Wales website (www.ccw.gov.uk) provides updated information on any closures.

Published by
Kittiwake
3 Glantwymyn Village Workshops, Glantwymyn, Machynlleth, Montgomeryshire SY20 8LY

© Text and map research: David Berry 2006
© Maps & illustrations: Kittiwake 2006
Drawings by Morag Perrott

Cover photographs by David Berry:
large: The River Clwyd (**Walk 8**): *inset*: Denbigh Castle (**Walk 6**)

Care has been taken to be accurate.
However neither the author nor the publisher can accept responsibility for any errors which may appear, or their consequences. If you are in any doubt about access, check before you proceed.

Printed by MWL, Pontypool.
First edition: 2000
Reprint with amendments: 2002. New extended edition 2006, reprinted 2007, 2008, 2009.

ISBN: 978 **1 902302 37 9**